Cognitive Distortions, Bias and Fallacies

Cognitive Distortions, Bias and Fallacies

Edited by:
Harvey Norris, MSW, LCSW

TURTLE PRESS

Library of Congress Cataloging in
Publication Data

Norris, Harvey S.

This book is dedicated to my wife,

Marguerite, who saw something in me

even when I could not see it in myself.

Thanks for 22 years and five children

What is a Flash Card Book?

Simply, a book organized like flashcards. You can use it as flashcards, as a reference or take it to your local print and copy shop and have them cut the binding off, leaving you with flashcards you can shuffle.

It is a simple way to produce and distribute flashcards easily without loss or high overhead.

Why Cognitive Distortions?

I started study distortions seriously about 8 years ago. As therapists, we are familiar with Ego Defense Mechanisms, which are like cognitive distortions on steroids. But, distortions, fallacies and biases are much more subtle. Often we run into a client using a distortion and we "know" it is wrong, but do not know how to "capture it ... define it" so we can help the client see the problem. Once you can name things and define them, it becomes easier to talk about them.

Years ago I worked with a young man who was involved in the Juvenile Justice System. He stated that *"all cops are bad!"* This statement is factually incorrect. But when I tried to point out there were good cops, the response I got back was *"all the cops I know are bad!"*

This was a circular argument which went several levels deep and became a problem. When I was able to define his statements/ behavior as a "Fallacy of Composition", where a person takes information about a part of a system and stretches it to cover the whole system, I was able to confront his distortion in a more therapeutic manner.

Instead of saying, "I think you are wrong, mistaken or misunderstanding, I was able to say, -- you have just committed a *Fallacy of Composition!*   I Then explained it to him, and now he had a framework in which to perceive his behaviors.

His respond was, *"Well, I don't like cops!"*

This is an honest statement that takes responsibility for behavior and can be therapeutically engaged. He was able to perceive the power and control he had when labeling and defining people.

This is when I understood that more people had to be able to define these issues.

This Flash Card Book is the beginning of that project.

I hope to follow with a more extensive work detailing statements and inferences from many of the fallacies and biases presented in this work.

As always, please provide me feedback, requests and information at

harveynorris@yahoo.com

Kindest Regards,

Available at

Available at

Available at

Ambiguity effect

☐ Completed

Card - 1

COGNITIVE DISTORTIONS

Attentional Bias

☐ Completed

Card - 2

COGNITIVE DISTORTIONS

Availability heuristic

☐ Completed

Card - 3

the tendency to avoid options for which missing information makes the probability seem "unknown."

COGNITIVE DISTORTIONS

the tendency of emotionally dominant stimuli in one's environment to preferentially draw and hold attention and to neglect relevant data when making judgments of a correlation or association.

COGNITIVE DISTORTIONS

estimating what is more likely by what is more available in memory, which is biased toward vivid, unusual, or emotionally charged examples.

□ Completed

Availability cascade

Card - 4

COGNITIVE DISTORTIONS

□ Completed

Backfire effect

Card - 5

COGNITIVE DISTORTIONS

□ Completed

Bandwagon effect

Card - 6

a self-reinforcing process in which a collective belief gains more and more plausibility through its increasing repetition in public discourse (or "repeat something long enough and it will become true").

COGNITIVE DISTORTIONS

when people react to disconfirming evidence by strengthening their beliefs.

COGNITIVE DISTORTIONS

the tendency to do (or believe) things because many other people do (or believe) the same. Related to groupthink and herd behavior.

☐ Completed

Base rate fallacy

Card - 7

COGNITIVE DISTORTIONS

☐ Completed

Belief bias

Card - 8

COGNITIVE DISTORTIONS

☐ Completed

Bias blind spot

Card - 9

the tendency to base judgments on specifics, ignoring general statistical information.

COGNITIVE DISTORTIONS

an effect where someone's evaluation of the logical strength of an argument is biased by the believability of the conclusion.

COGNITIVE DISTORTIONS

the tendency to see oneself as less biased than other people, or to be able to identify more cognitive biases in others than in oneself.

☐ Completed

Choice-supportive bias

Card - 10

COGNITIVE DISTORTIONS

☐ Completed

Clustering illusion

Card - 11

COGNITIVE DISTORTIONS

☐ Completed

Confirmation bias

Card - 12

the tendency to remember one's choices as better than they actually were.

the tendency to under-expect runs, streaks or clusters in small samples of random data

the tendency to search for or interpret information in a way that confirms one's preconceptions.

Congruence bias

Card - 13

COGNITIVE DISTORTIONS

Conjunction fallacy

Card - 14

COGNITIVE DISTORTIONS

Conservatism

or

Regressive Bias

Card - 15

the tendency to test hypotheses exclusively through direct testing, in contrast to tests of possible alternative hypotheses.

COGNITIVE DISTORTIONS

the tendency to assume that specific conditions are more probable than general ones.

COGNITIVE DISTORTIONS

tendency to underestimate high values and high likelihoods/probabilities/frequencies and overestimate low ones. Based on the observed evidence, estimates are not extreme enough

Conservatism (Bayesian)

☐ Completed

Card - 16

COGNITIVE DISTORTIONS

Contrast effect

☐ Completed

Card - 17

COGNITIVE DISTORTIONS

Curse of knowledge

☐ Completed

Card - 18

tendency to belief update insufficiently but predictably as a result of new evidence (estimates of conditional probabilities are conservative)

COGNITIVE DISTORTIONS

the enhancement or diminishing of a weight or other measurement when compared with a recently observed contrasting object.

COGNITIVE DISTORTIONS

when better-informed people lose the ability to understand lesser-informed people

Decoy effect

☐ Completed

Card - 19

COGNITIVE DISTORTIONS

Denomination effect

☐ Completed

Card - 20

COGNITIVE DISTORTIONS

Distinction bias

☐ Completed

Card - 21

preferences change when there is a third option that is asymmetrically dominated

COGNITIVE DISTORTIONS

the tendency to spend more money when it is denominated in small amounts (e.g. coins) rather than large amounts (e.g. bills).

COGNITIVE DISTORTIONS

the tendency to view two options as more dissimilar when evaluating them simultaneously than when evaluating them separately.

Duration neglect

Card - 22

COGNITIVE DISTORTIONS

Empathy gap

Card - 23

COGNITIVE DISTORTIONS

Endowment effect

Card - 24

The neglect of the duration of an episode in determining its value

the tendency to underestimate the influence or strength of feelings, in either oneself or others.

the fact that people often demand much more to give up an object than they would be willing to pay to acquire it.

□ Completed

Essentialism

Card - 25

COGNITIVE DISTORTIONS

□ Completed

Exaggerated expectation

Card - 26

COGNITIVE DISTORTIONS

□ Completed

Experimenter's

or

Expectation bias

Card - 27

categorizing people and things according to their essential nature, in spite of variations.

COGNITIVE DISTORTIONS

based on the estimates, real-world evidence turns out to be less extreme than our expectations (conditionally inverse of the conservatism bias).

COGNITIVE DISTORTIONS

The tendency for experimenters to believe, certify, and publish data that agree with their expectations for the outcome of an experiment, and to disbelieve, discard, or downgrade the corresponding weightings for data that appear to conflict with those expectations.

□ Completed

Functional fixedness

Card - 28

COGNITIVE DISTORTIONS

□ Completed

Focusing effect

Card - 29

COGNITIVE DISTORTIONS

□ Completed

Framing effect

Card - 30

limits a person to using an object only in the way it is traditionally used

COGNITIVE DISTORTIONS

the tendency to place too much importance on one aspect of an event; causes error in accurately predicting the utility of a future outcome.

COGNITIVE DISTORTIONS

drawing different conclusions from the same information, depending on how that information is presented.

□ Completed

Frequency illusion

Card - 31

COGNITIVE DISTORTIONS

□ Completed

Gambler's fallacy

Card - 32

COGNITIVE DISTORTIONS

□ Completed

Hard-easy effect

Card - 33

the illusion in which a word, a name or other thing that has recently come to one's attention suddenly appears "everywhere" with improbable frequency (see also recency illusion).

COGNITIVE DISTORTIONS

the tendency to think that future probabilities are altered by past events, when in reality they are unchanged. Results from an erroneous conceptualization of the Law of large numbers. *For example, "I've flipped heads with this coin five times consecutively, so the chance of tails coming out on the sixth flip is much greater than heads."*

COGNITIVE DISTORTIONS

Based on a specific level of task difficulty, the confidence in judgments is too conservative and not extreme enough

Hindsight bias

Card - 34

COGNITIVE DISTORTIONS

Hostile media effect

Card - 35

COGNITIVE DISTORTIONS

Hyperbolic discounting

Card - 36

☐ Completed

☐ Completed

☐ Completed

sometimes called the "I-knew-it-all-along" effect, the tendency to see past events as being predictable at the time those events happened.

(sometimes phrased as "Hindsight is 20/20")

COGNITIVE DISTORTIONS

the tendency to see a media report as being biased due to one's own strong partisan views.

COGNITIVE DISTORTIONS

the tendency for people to have a stronger preference for more immediate payoffs relative to later payoffs, where the tendency increases the closer to the present both payoffs are.

☐ Completed

Illusion of control

Card - 37

COGNITIVE DISTORTIONS

☐ Completed

Illusion of validity

Card - 38

COGNITIVE DISTORTIONS

☐ Completed

Illusory correlation

Card - 39

the tendency to overestimate one's degree of influence over other external events.

when consistent but predicatively weak data leads to confident predictions

inaccurately perceiving a relationship between two unrelated events.

☐ Completed

Impact bias

Card - 40

☐ Completed

Information bias

Card - 41

☐ Completed

Insensitivity to sample size

Card - 42

the tendency to overestimate the length or the intensity of the impact of future feeling states.

the tendency to seek information even when it cannot affect action.

the tendency to under-expect variation in small samples

□ Completed

Pareidolia

Card - 43

COGNITIVE DISTORTIONS

□ Completed

Jealousy bias

Card - 44

COGNITIVE DISTORTIONS

□ Completed

Just-world hypothesis

Card - 45

a vague and random stimulus (often an image or sound) is perceived as significant, e.g., seeing images of animals or faces in clouds, the man in the moon, and hearing hidden messages on records played in reverse.

COGNITIVE DISTORTIONS

a tendency to have persistent paranoid thoughts about a "mate poacher" and/or personal inadequacies in comparison to someone else. The irrational thoughts disrupt environments and routines because the bias creates compulsions.

COGNITIVE DISTORTIONS

the tendency for people to want to believe that the world is fundamentally just, causing them to rationalize an otherwise inexplicable injustice as deserved by the victim(s).

Knowledge bias

COGNITIVE DISTORTIONS

☐ Completed

Less-is-better effect

COGNITIVE DISTORTIONS

☐ Completed

Loss aversion

the tendency of people to choose the option they know best rather than the best option.

COGNITIVE DISTORTIONS

a preference reversal where a dominated smaller set is preferred to a larger set

COGNITIVE DISTORTIONS

"the disutility of giving up an object is greater than the utility associated with acquiring it".

☐ Completed

Mere exposure effect

Card - 49

☐ Completed

Money illusion

Card - 50

☐ Completed

Moral credential effect

Card - 51

the tendency to express undue liking for things merely because of familiarity with them.

the tendency to concentrate on the nominal (face value) of money rather than its value in terms of purchasing power.

the tendency of a track record of non-prejudice to increase subsequent prejudice.

Negativity bias

Card - 52

COGNITIVE DISTORTIONS

Neglect of probability

Card - 53

COGNITIVE DISTORTIONS

Normalcy bias

Card - 54

the tendency to pay more attention and give more weight to negative than positive experiences or other kinds of information.

COGNITIVE DISTORTIONS

the tendency to completely disregard probability when making a decision under uncertainty.

COGNITIVE DISTORTIONS

the refusal to plan for, or react to, a disaster which has never happened before.

☐ Completed

Observer-expectancy

effect

Card - 55

COGNITIVE DISTORTIONS

☐ Completed

Omission bias

Card - 56

COGNITIVE DISTORTIONS

☐ Completed

Optimism bias

Card - 57

when a researcher expects a given result and therefore unconsciously manipulates an experiment or misinterprets data in order to find it (see also subject-expectancy effect).

COGNITIVE DISTORTIONS

the tendency to judge harmful actions as worse, or less moral, than equally harmful omissions (inactions).

COGNITIVE DISTORTIONS

the tendency to be over-optimistic, overestimating favorable and pleasing outcomes (see also wishful thinking, valence effect, positive outcome bias).

□ Completed

Ostrich effect

Card - 58

COGNITIVE DISTORTIONS

□ Completed

Outcome bias

Card - 59

COGNITIVE DISTORTIONS

□ Completed

Overconfidence effect

Card - 60

ignoring an obvious (negative) situation.

COGNITIVE DISTORTIONS

the tendency to judge a decision by its eventual outcome instead of based on the quality of the decision at the time it was made.

COGNITIVE DISTORTIONS

excessive confidence in one's own answers to questions. For example, for certain types of questions, answers that people rate as "99% certain" turn out to be wrong 40% of the time.

□ Completed

Always being right

Card - 61

COGNITIVE DISTORTIONS

□ Completed

Planning fallacy

Card - 62

COGNITIVE DISTORTIONS

□ Completed

Post-purchase rationalization

Card - 63

Being wrong is unthinkable and we will go to any length to demonstrate our rightness. Being right often is more important than the feelings of others around a person who engages in this cognitive distortion, even loved ones.

COGNITIVE DISTORTIONS

the tendency to underestimate task-completion times.

COGNITIVE DISTORTIONS

the tendency to persuade oneself through rational argument that a purchase was a good value.

☐ Completed

Actor-observer bias

Card - 64

COGNITIVE DISTORTIONS

☐ Completed

Pseudocertainty effect

Card - 65

COGNITIVE DISTORTIONS

☐ Completed

Reactance

Card - 66

the tendency for explanations of other individuals' behaviors to overemphasize the influence of their personality and underemphasize the influence of their situation

COGNITIVE DISTORTIONS

the tendency to make risk-averse choices if the expected outcome is positive, but make risk-seeking choices to avoid negative outcomes.

COGNITIVE DISTORTIONS

the urge to do the opposite of what someone wants you to do out of a need to resist a perceived attempt to constrain your freedom of choice

□ Completed

Reactive devaluation

Card - 67

COGNITIVE DISTORTIONS

□ Completed

Recency bias

Card - 68

COGNITIVE DISTORTIONS

□ Completed

Recency illusion

Card - 69

devaluing proposals that are no longer hypothetical or purportedly originated with an adversary

COGNITIVE DISTORTIONS

a cognitive bias that results from disproportionate salience of recent stimuli or observations – the tendency to weigh recent events more than earlier events

COGNITIVE DISTORTIONS

– the illusion that a phenomenon, typically a word or language usage, that one has just begun to notice is a recent innovation (see also frequency illusion).

□ Completed

Restraint bias

Card - 70

COGNITIVE DISTORTIONS

□ Completed

Rhyme as reason effect

Card - 71

COGNITIVE DISTORTIONS

□ Completed

Selective perception

Card - 72

– the tendency to overestimate one's ability to show restraint in the face of temptation.

COGNITIVE DISTORTIONS

– rhyming statements are perceived as more truthful.

COGNITIVE DISTORTIONS

– the tendency for expectations to affect perception.

□ Completed

Semmelweis reflex

Card - 73

□ Completed

Social comparison bias

Card - 74

□ Completed

Social desirability bias

Card - 75

– the tendency to reject new evidence that contradicts a paradigm.

COGNITIVE DISTORTIONS

– the tendency, when making hiring decisions, to favor potential candidates who do not compete with one's own particular strengths.

COGNITIVE DISTORTIONS

- the tendency to over-report socially desirable characteristics or behaviors and under-report socially undesirable characteristics or behaviors.

□ Completed

Status quo bias

Card - 76

COGNITIVE DISTORTIONS

□ Completed

Stereotyping

Card - 77

COGNITIVE DISTORTIONS

□ Completed

Subadditivity effect

Card - 78

– the tendency to like things to stay relatively the same (see also loss aversion, endowment effect, and system justification).

COGNITIVE DISTORTIONS

– expecting a member of a group to have certain characteristics without having actual information about that individual.

COGNITIVE DISTORTIONS

– the tendency to estimate that the likelihood of an event is less than the sum of its (more than two) mutually exclusive components.

☐ Completed

Subjective validation

Card - 79

COGNITIVE DISTORTIONS

☐ Completed

Time-saving bias

Card - 80

COGNITIVE DISTORTIONS

☐ Completed

Unit bias

Card - 81

– perception that something is true if a subject's belief demands it to be true. Also assigns perceived connections between coincidences.

– underestimations of the time that could be saved (or lost) when increasing (or decreasing) from a relatively low speed and overestimations of the time that could be saved (or lost) when increasing (or decreasing) from a relatively high speed.

– the tendency to want to finish a given unit of a task or an item. Strong effects on the consumption of food in particular.

☐ Completed

Appeal to ignorance

Card - 82

COGNITIVE DISTORTIONS

☐ Completed

Zero-risk bias

Card - 83

COGNITIVE DISTORTIONS

☐ Completed

Zeigarnik effect

Card - 84

Claim X is presented by side A and the burden of proof actually rests on side B.

Side B claims that X is false because there is no proof for X

COGNITIVE DISTORTIONS

– preference for reducing a small risk to zero over a greater reduction in a larger risk.

COGNITIVE DISTORTIONS

that uncompleted or interrupted tasks are remembered better than completed ones.

□ Completed

Begging the question

Card - 85

□ Completed

Blaming

Card - 86

□ Completed

Catastrophizing

Card - 87

demonstrates a conclusion by means of premises that assume that conclusion.
(2) The premise and the conclusion have the same meaning. If one has already accepted the premise, there is no need to reason to the conclusion.

COGNITIVE DISTORTIONS

We hold other people responsible for our pain, or take the other track and blame ourselves for every problem.

COGNITIVE DISTORTIONS

Inability to foresee anything other than the worst possible outcome, however unlikely, or experiencing a situation as unbearable or impossible when it is just uncomfortable.

☐ Completed

Childhood amnesia

Card - 88

COGNITIVE DISTORTIONS

☐ Completed

Connotation fallacies

Card - 89

COGNITIVE DISTORTIONS

☐ Completed

Consistency bias

Card - 90

the retention of few memories from before the age of four

occur when a dysphemistic word is substituted for the speaker's actual quote and used to discredit the argument. It is a form of attribution fallacy.

incorrectly remembering one's past attitudes and behavior as resembling present attitudes and behavior.

☐ Completed

Context effect

Card - 91

COGNITIVE DISTORTIONS

☐ Completed

Cross-race effect

Card - 92

COGNITIVE DISTORTIONS

☐ Completed

Cryptomnesia

Card - 93

that cognition and memory are dependent on context, such that out-of-context memories are more difficult to retrieve than in-context memories (e.g., recall time and accuracy for a work-related memory will be lower at home, and vice versa)

COGNITIVE DISTORTIONS

the tendency for people of one race to have difficulty identifying members of a race other than their own

COGNITIVE DISTORTIONS

a form of misattribution where a memory is mistaken for imagination, because there is no subjective experience of it being a memory.

□ Completed

Defensive attribution hypothesis

Card - 94

□ Completed

Denying the antecedent

Card - 95

□ Completed

Disqualifying the positive

Card - 96

defensive attributions are made when individuals witness or learn of a mishap happening to another person. In these situations, attributions of responsibility to the victim or harm-doer for the mishap will depend upon the severity of the outcomes of the mishap and the level of personal and situational similarity between the individual and victim.

COGNITIVE DISTORTIONS

If it is raining outside, it must be cloudy. It is not raining outside. Therefore, it is not cloudy.
Problem: Rain is a sufficient condition of cloudiness, but cloudy conditions do not

COGNITIVE DISTORTIONS

Discounting positive experiences for arbitrary, ad hoc reasons.

□ Completed

Dunning–Kruger effect

Card - 97

COGNITIVE DISTORTIONS

□ Completed

Egocentric bias

Card - 98

COGNITIVE DISTORTIONS

□ Completed

Egocentric bias

Card - 99

an effect in which incompetent people fail to realize they are incompetent because they lack the skill to distinguish between competence and incompetence

COGNITIVE DISTORTIONS

occurs when people claim more responsibility for themselves for the results of a joint action than an outside observer would.

COGNITIVE DISTORTIONS

recalling the past in a self-serving manner, e.g., remembering one's exam grades as being better than they were, or remembering a caught fish as bigger than it really was

☐ Completed

Emotional Reasoning

Card - 100

COGNITIVE DISTORTIONS

☐ Completed

External
Control
Fallacies

Card - 101

COGNITIVE DISTORTIONS

☐ Completed

Equivocation

Card - 102

Experiencing reality as a reflection of emotions, e.g. "I feel it, therefore it must be true."   If we feel stupid and boring, then we must be stupid and boring. You assume that your unhealthy emotions reflect the way things really are — "I feel it, therefore it must be true."

COGNITIVE DISTORTIONS

If we feel externally controlled, we see ourselves as helpless a victim of fate.
example, "I can't help it if the quality of the work is poor, my boss demanded I work overtime on it."

COGNITIVE DISTORTIONS

consists in employing the same word in two or more senses, e.g. in a syllogism, the middle term being used in one sense in the major and another in the minor premise, so that in fact there are four not three terms. Often this happens when the two meanings are similar despite being distinctly different.

Completed

Fading affect bias

Card - 103

COGNITIVE DISTORTIONS

 Completed

Fallacy of accident
or
sweeping generalization

Card - 104

COGNITIVE DISTORTIONS

 Completed

Converse fallacy of accident

Card - 105

a bias in which the emotion associated with unpleasant memories fades more quickly than the emotion associated with positive events.

COGNITIVE DISTORTIONS

a generalization that disregards exceptions.

Example: Cutting people is a crime. Surgeons cut people, therefore, surgeons are criminals

COGNITIVE DISTORTIONS

or hasty generalization argues from a special case to a general rule.

☐ Completed

Fallacy of Change

Card - 106

COGNITIVE DISTORTIONS

☐ Completed

Fallacy of composition

Card - 107

COGNITIVE DISTORTIONS

☐ Completed

Fallacy of Fairness

Card - 108

We expect that other people will change to suit us if we just pressure or cajole them enough. We need to change people because our hopes for happiness seem to depend entirely on them.

COGNITIVE DISTORTIONS

Arguing from some property of constituent parts, to the conclusion that the composite item has that property. Example Argument: All the musicians in a band (constituent parts) are highly skilled, therefore the band itself (composite item) is highly skilled. Problem: The band members may be skilled musicians but may lack the ability to function properly as a group.

COGNITIVE DISTORTIONS

We feel resentful because we think we know what is fair, but other people won't agree with us. As our parents tell us, "Life is always fair," and people who go through life applying a measuring ruler against every situation judging its "fairness" will often feel badly and negative because of it.

☐ Completed

Fallacy of false cause

Card - 109

☐ Completed

Post hoc ergo propter hoc

Card - 110

☐ Completed

indication of causation

Card - 111

incorrectly assumes one thing is the cause of another. Non Sequitur is Latin for "It does not follow."

COGNITIVE DISTORTIONS

believing that temporal succession implies a causal relation.

COGNITIVE DISTORTIONS

believing that correlation implies a causal relation.

☐ Completed

Fallacy of many questions

Card - 112

COGNITIVE DISTORTIONS

☐ Completed

False consensus effect

Card - 113

COGNITIVE DISTORTIONS

☐ Completed

False memory

Card - 114

groups more than one question in the form of a single question.

Argument: Have you stopped beating your wife?

the tendency for people to overestimate the degree to which others agree with them.

a form of misattribution where imagination is mistaken for a memory.

☐ Completed

Figure of Speech

Card - 115

COGNITIVE DISTORTIONS

☐ Completed

Filtering

Card - 116

COGNITIVE DISTORTIONS

☐ Completed

Barnum effect

Card - 117

the confusion between the metaphorical or figurative use of a word or phrase and the ordinary or literal use of a word or phrase.

COGNITIVE DISTORTIONS

take the negative details and magnify them while filtering out all positive aspects of a situation.

COGNITIVE DISTORTIONS

the tendency to give high accuracy ratings to descriptions of their personality that supposedly are tailored specifically for them, but are in fact vague and general enough to apply to a wide range of people.

☐ Completed

Fortune telling

Card - 118

☐ Completed

Fundamental attribution error

Card - 119

☐ Completed

Generation effect (Self-generation effect)

Card - 120

Inflexible expectations for how things will turn out before they happen.

COGNITIVE DISTORTIONS

the tendency for people to over-emphasize personality-based explanations for behaviors observed in others while under-emphasizing the role and power of situational influences on the same behavior

COGNITIVE DISTORTIONS

that self-generated information is remembered best. For instance, people are better able to recall memories of statements that they have generated than similar statements generated by others.

□ Completed

Google effect

Card - 121

COGNITIVE DISTORTIONS

□ Completed

Halo effect

Card - 122

COGNITIVE DISTORTIONS

□ Completed

Illusion of asymmetric insight

Card - 123

the tendency to forget information that can be easily found online.

COGNITIVE DISTORTIONS

the tendency for a person's positive or negative traits to "spill over" from one area of their personality to another in others' perceptions of them

COGNITIVE DISTORTIONS

people perceive their knowledge of their peers to surpass their peers' knowledge of them.

Hasty generalization

☐ Completed

Card - 124

Heaven's Reward Fallacy

☐ Completed

Card - 125

Humor effect

☐ Completed

Card - 126

is the fallacy of examining just one or very few examples or studying a single case, and generalizing that to be representative of the whole class of objects or phenomena.

COGNITIVE DISTORTIONS

We expect our sacrifice and self-denial to pay off, as if someone is keeping score. We feel bitter when the reward doesn't come.

COGNITIVE DISTORTIONS

that humorous items are more easily remembered than non -humorous ones, which might be explained by the distinctiveness of humor, the increased cognitive processing time to understand the humor, or the emotional arousal caused by the humor.

□ Completed

Illusion of external agency

Card - 127

□ Completed

Illusion of transparency

Card - 128

□ Completed

Illusion-of-truth effect

Card - 129

when people view self-generated preferences as
instead being caused by insightful, effective and
benevolent agents

COGNITIVE DISTORTIONS

people overestimate others' ability to know them, and
they also overestimate their ability to know others.

COGNITIVE DISTORTIONS

that people are more likely to identify as true statements
those they have previously heard (even if they cannot
consciously remember having heard them), regardless of
the actual validity of the statement. In other words, a
person is more likely to believe a familiar statement than
an unfamiliar one.

☐ Completed

Illusory superiority

Card - 130

COGNITIVE DISTORTIONS

☐ Completed

Anchoring

Card - 131

COGNITIVE DISTORTIONS

☐ Completed

Information bias

Card - 132

overestimating one's desirable qualities, and underestimating undesirable qualities, relative to other people.

COGNITIVE DISTORTIONS

the tendency to rely too heavily, or "anchor," on a past reference or on one trait or piece of information when making decisions (also called "insufficient adjustment")

COGNITIVE DISTORTIONS

the tendency to seek information even when it cannot affect action.

□ Completed

Ingroup bias

Card - 133

COGNITIVE DISTORTIONS

□ Completed

Just-world phenomenon

Card - 134

COGNITIVE DISTORTIONS

□ Completed

Internal Control Fallacies

Card - 135

the tendency for people to give preferential treatment to others they perceive to be members of their own groups.

COGNITIVE DISTORTIONS

the tendency for people to believe that the world is just and therefore people "get what they deserve."

COGNITIVE DISTORTIONS

The fallacy of internal control has us assuming responsibility for the pain and happiness of everyone around us.

□ Completed

Irrational escalation

Card - 136

COGNITIVE DISTORTIONS

□ Completed

Irrelevant conclusion

Card - 137

COGNITIVE DISTORTIONS

□ Completed

Jumping to Conclusions

Card - 138

the phenomenon where people justify increased investment in a decision, based on the cumulative prior investment, despite new evidence suggesting that the decision was probably wrong.

COGNITIVE DISTORTIONS

diverts attention away from a fact in dispute rather than addressing it directly.

COGNITIVE DISTORTIONS

Without individuals saying so, we know what they are feeling and why they act the way they do. In particular, we are able to determine how people are feeling toward us.

☐ Completed

Labeling and mislabeling

Card - 139

COGNITIVE DISTORTIONS

☐ Completed

Leveling and Sharpening

Card - 140

COGNITIVE DISTORTIONS

☐ Completed

Levels-of-processing effect

Card - 141

Limited thinking about behaviors or events due to reliance on names. Rather than describing the specific behavior, the person assigns a label to someone or himself that implies absolute and unalterable terms.

COGNITIVE DISTORTIONS

memory distortions introduced by the loss of details in a recollection over time, often concurrent with sharpening or selective recollection of certain details that take on exaggerated significance in relation to the details or aspects of the experience lost through leveling. Both biases may be reinforced over time, and by repeated recollection or re-telling of a memory.

COGNITIVE DISTORTIONS

that different methods of encoding information into memory have different levels of effectiveness

□ Completed

Magical thinking

Card - 142

□ Completed

Magnification and minimization

Card - 143

□ Completed

Mental filter

Card - 144

Expectation of certain outcomes based on performance of unrelated acts or utterances.

COGNITIVE DISTORTIONS

Magnifying or minimizing a memory or situation such that they no longer correspond to objective reality. This is common enough in the normal population to popularize idioms such as "make a mountain out of a molehill." In depressed clients, often the positive characteristics of other people are exaggerated and negative characteristics are understated.

COGNITIVE DISTORTIONS

Inability to view positive or negative features of an experience, for example, noticing only a tiny imperfection in a piece of otherwise useful clothing. (A memory bias)

☐ Completed

Mind reading

Card - 145

☐ Completed

Misattribution

Card - 146

☐ Completed

Misinformation effect

Card - 147

Sense of access to special knowledge of the intentions or thoughts of others.

(A memory bias)

COGNITIVE DISTORTIONS

when information is retained in memory but the source of the memory is forgotten.

(A memory bias)

COGNITIVE DISTORTIONS

that misinformation affects people's reports of their own memory.

(A memory bias)

□ Completed

Misleading vividness

Card - 148

□ Completed

Modality effect

Card - 149

□ Completed

Mood congruent memory bias

Card - 150

is a kind of hasty generalization that appeals to the senses.

(A memory bias)

COGNITIVE DISTORTIONS

that memory recall is higher for the last items of a list when the list items were received via speech than when they were received via writing.

(A memory bias)

COGNITIVE DISTORTIONS

the improved recall of information congruent with one's current mood.

(A memory bias)

☐ Completed

Global labeling

Card - 151

☐ Completed

Naive cynicism

Card - 152

☐ Completed

Moral luck

Card - 153

We generalize one or two qualities into a negative global judgment. These are extreme forms of generalizing, and are also referred to as "labeling" and "mislabeling." Instead of describing an error in context of a specific situation, a person will attach an unhealthy label to themselves.

COGNITIVE DISTORTIONS

expecting more egocentric bias in other than in oneself

COGNITIVE DISTORTIONS

the tendency for people to ascribe greater or lesser moral standing based on the outcome of an event rather than the intention

Next-in-line effect

Card - 154

COGNITIVE DISTORTIONS

Osborn effect

Card - 155

COGNITIVE DISTORTIONS

Outgroup homogeneity bias

Card - 156

that a person in a group has diminished recall for the words of others who spoke immediately before or after this person.

COGNITIVE DISTORTIONS

that being intoxicated with a mind-altering substance makes it harder to retrieve motor patterns from the Basal Ganglion.

COGNITIVE DISTORTIONS

individuals see members of their own group as being relatively more varied than members of other groups.

☐ Completed

Overgeneralization

Card - 157

☐ Completed

overwhelming exception

Card - 158

☐ Completed

Part-list cueing effect

Card - 159

we come to a general conclusion based on a single incident or a single piece of evidence.

COGNITIVE DISTORTIONS

a generalization which is accurate, but tags on a qualification which eliminates enough cases (as exceptions); that what remains is much less impressive than what the original statement might have led one to assume

COGNITIVE DISTORTIONS

that being shown some items from a list makes it harder to retrieve the other items

☐ Completed

Peak-end rule

Card - 160

COGNITIVE DISTORTIONS

☐ Completed

Personalization

Card - 161

COGNITIVE DISTORTIONS

☐ Completed

Pessimism bias

Card - 162

that people seem to perceive not the sum of an experience but the average of how it was at its peak (e.g. pleasant or unpleasant) and how it ended.

COGNITIVE DISTORTIONS

a distortion where a person believes that everything others do or say is some kind of direct, personal reaction to the person.

example, "We were late to the dinner party and caused the hostess to overcook the meal. If I had only pushed my husband to leave on time, this wouldn't have happened."

COGNITIVE DISTORTIONS

the tendency for some people, especially those suffering from depression, to overestimate the likelihood of negative things happening to them.

☐ Completed

Picture superiority effect

Card - 163

COGNITIVE DISTORTIONS

☐ Completed

Placement bias

Card - 164

COGNITIVE DISTORTIONS

☐ Completed

Polarized Thinking

Card - 165

that concepts are much more likely to be remembered experientially if they are presented in picture form than if they are presented in word form.

COGNITIVE DISTORTIONS

tendency to remember ourselves to be better than others at tasks at which we rate ourselves above average (also Illusory superiority or Better-than-average effect) and tendency to remember ourselves to be worse than others at tasks at which we rate ourselves below average (also Worse-than-average effect

COGNITIVE DISTORTIONS

things are either "black-or-white." We have to be perfect or we're a failure — there is no middle ground. If your performance falls short of perfect, you see yourself as a total failure.

Positivity effect

Card - 166

COGNITIVE DISTORTIONS

Primacy effect

Card - 167

COGNITIVE DISTORTIONS

Pro-innovation bias

Card - 168

that older adults favor positive over negative Information in their memories.

COGNITIVE DISTORTIONS

that items near the end of a list are the easiest to recall, followed by the items at the beginning of a list; items in the middle are the least likely to be remembered.

COGNITIVE DISTORTIONS

the tendency to reflect a personal bias towards an invention/innovation, while often failing to identify limitations and weaknesses or address the possibility of failure

☐ Completed

Projection bias

Card - 169

☐ Completed

Proof by verbosity

Card - 170

☐ Completed

verbosum

Card - 171

the tendency to unconsciously assume that others (or one's future selves) share one's current emotional states, thoughts and values.

COGNITIVE DISTORTIONS

Proof by verbosity, sometimes colloquially referred to as argumentum

COGNITIVE DISTORTIONS

a rhetorical technique that tries to persuade by overwhelming those considering an argument with such a volume of material that the argument sounds plausible, superficially appears to be well-researched, and it is so laborious to untangle and check supporting facts that the argument might be allowed to slide by unchallenged.

☐ Completed

Reminiscence bump

Card - 172

☐ Completed

Rosy retrospection

Card - 173

☐ Completed

List length effect

Card - 174

the recalling of more personal events from adolescence and early adulthood than personal events from other lifetime periods

COGNITIVE DISTORTIONS

the remembering of the past as having been better than it really was.

COGNITIVE DISTORTIONS

a smaller percentage of items are remembered in a longer list, but as the length of the list increases, the absolute number of items remembered increases as well.

☐ Completed

Self-relevance effect

Card - 175

☐ Completed

Self-serving bias

Card - 176

☐ Completed

Should statements

Card - 177

that memories relating to the self are better recalled than similar information relating to others.

COGNITIVE DISTORTIONS

perceiving oneself responsible for desirable outcomes but not responsible for undesirable ones.

COGNITIVE DISTORTIONS

Patterns of thought which imply the way things "should" or "ought" to be rather than the actual situation the person is faced with, or having rigid rules which the person believes will "always apply" no matter what the circumstances are. People who break the rules make us angry, and we feel guilty when we violate these rules.

□ Completed

Slothful induction

Card - 178

COGNITIVE DISTORTIONS

□ Completed

Persistence

Card - 179

COGNITIVE DISTORTIONS

□ Completed

Tip-of-the-tongue phenomenon

Card - 180

The opposite of hasty generalization, is the fallacy of denying the logical conclusion of an inductive argument, dismissing an effect as "just a coincidence" when it is very likely not to be

COGNITIVE DISTORTIONS

the unwanted recurrence of memories of a traumatic event.

COGNITIVE DISTORTIONS

when a subject is able to recall parts of an item, or related information, but is frustratingly unable to recall the whole item.

□ Completed

Source Confusion

Card - 181

COGNITIVE DISTORTIONS

□ Completed

Genetic fallacy

Card - 182

COGNITIVE DISTORTIONS

□ Completed

Stereotyping

Card - 183

misattributing the source of a memory, e.g. misremembering that one saw an event personally when actually it was seen on television.

COGNITIVE DISTORTIONS

a line of "reasoning" in which a perceived defect in the origin of a claim or thing is taken to be evidence that discredits the claim or thing itself. It is also a line of reasoning in which the origin of a claim or thing is taken to be evidence for the claim or thing.

COGNITIVE DISTORTIONS

expecting a member of a group to have certain characteristics without having actual information about that individual.

☐ Completed

Suffix effect

Card - 184

COGNITIVE DISTORTIONS

☐ Completed

Suggestibility

Card - 185

COGNITIVE DISTORTIONS

☐ Completed

System justification

Card - 186

the weakening of the recency effect in the case that an item is appended to the list that the subject is not required to recall

COGNITIVE DISTORTIONS

a form of misattribution where ideas suggested by a questioner are mistaken for memory.

COGNITIVE DISTORTIONS

the tendency to defend and bolster the status quo. Existing social, economic, and political arrangements tend to be preferred, and alternatives disparaged sometimes even at the expense of individual and collective self-interest.

Telescoping effect

COGNITIVE DISTORTIONS

Testing effect

COGNITIVE DISTORTIONS

Trait ascription bias

the tendency to displace recent events backward in time and remote events forward in time, so that recent events appear more remote, and remote events, more recent.

COGNITIVE DISTORTIONS

that frequent testing of material that has been committed to memory improves memory recall.

COGNITIVE DISTORTIONS

the tendency for people to view themselves as relatively variable in terms of personality, behavior, and mood while viewing others as much more predictable.

Ultimate attribution error

Card - 190

COGNITIVE DISTORTIONS

□ Completed

Verbatim effect

Card - 191

COGNITIVE DISTORTIONS

□ Completed

Von Restorff effect

Card - 192

similar to the fundamental attribution error, in this error a person is likely to make an internal attribution to an entire group instead of the individuals within the group.

COGNITIVE DISTORTIONS

that the "gist" of what someone has said is better remembered than the verbatim wording

COGNITIVE DISTORTIONS

that an item that sticks out is more likely to be remembered than other items

☐ Completed

Well travelled road effect

Card - 193

COGNITIVE DISTORTIONS

☐ Completed

Worse-than-average effect

Card - 194

COGNITIVE DISTORTIONS

underestimation of the duration taken to traverse oft-traveled routes and over-estimate the duration taken to traverse less familiar routes.

COGNITIVE DISTORTIONS

a tendency to believe ourselves to be worse than others at tasks which are difficult

COGNITIVE DISTORTIONS

Made in the USA
Las Vegas, NV
03 July 2023

74221756R00079